THE LITTLE BOOK OF

TENNIS

First published in 2025 by OH
An Imprint of HEADLINE PUBLISHING GROUP LIMITED

1

Disclaimer:

Cataloguing in Publication Data is available from the British Library

ISBN 978-1-03542-726-0

Compiled and written by: Malcolm Croft
Editorial: Saneaah Muhammad
Designed and typeset in Queulat by: Stephen Cary
Project manager: Russell Porter
Production: Rachel Burgess
Printed and bound in China

HEADLINE PUBLISHING GROUP LIMITED
An Hachette UK Company
Carmelite House, 50 Victoria Embankment, London EC4Y 0DZ

The authorised representative in the EEA is Hachette Ireland, 8 Castlecourt Centre,
Dublin 15, D15 XTP3, Ireland (email: info@hbgi.ie)

www.headline.co.uk   www.hachette.co.uk

THE LITTLE BOOK OF

TENNIS

SMASHING QUOTES

FROM THE GREATS OF THE GAME

CONTENTS

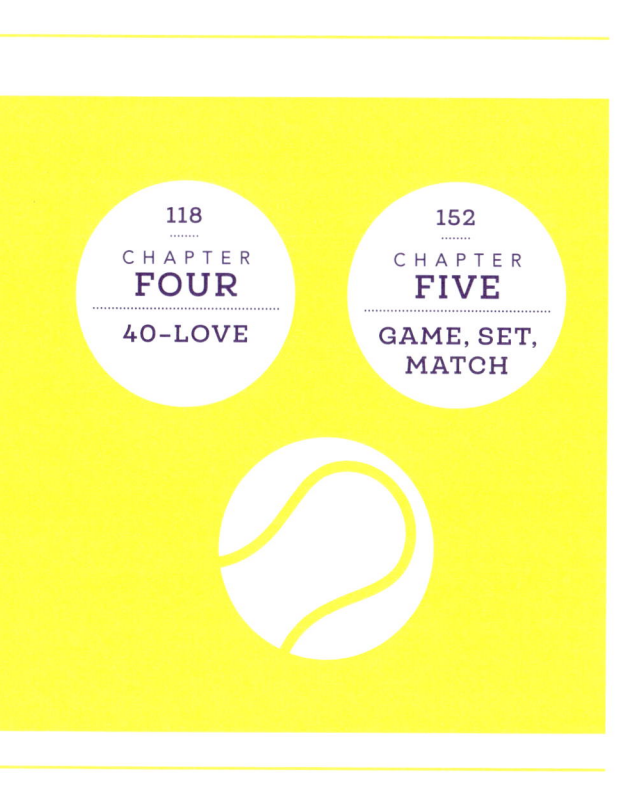

INTRODUCTION

Welcome to *The Little Book of Tennis*, a five-set thriller serving up a smashing celebration of the world's No. 1 court sport. Full of stats, facts, quotes, quips, icons and history, this treasure trove of trivia is the perfect love-all, a courtside companion that will soothe superfans from even the most severe bout of tennisitis, an addiction that the most loyal devotees of the game know all too well.

Since the founding of the Open Era in 1968, the original racquet game has evolved in front of our eyes beyond all recognition, the result of its ever-increasing global fame. The sport now has more than one billion fans worldwide – take that, squash! Today, tennis consistently remains a pioneer, not just of athletic endurance and lightning-fast reflexes, it's also big business, blazing trails for brands, TV, technology, fashion and media, with a litany of lucrative hustles. The game generates, and elevates, a new breed of sporting icons and inspirations every year too. From Agassi to Alcaraz, Graf to Gauff, Nadal to Navratilova, Sinner to Seles, Zverev to Zhizhen, tennis always delivers on its promise to promote next-level superstars that are never anything less than iconic. It produces more than its fair share of magical milestones, too. From Murray's 2013 Wimbledon win and McEnroe's 1981 court rant to a plethora of meltdowns, showdowns, rivalries, streakers – and anything that Nick Kyrgios does. Yes, there's never a dull moment in tennis.

Let's not dilly-dally any longer. It's tennis time. Pull up your socks and pick up your balls and get ready to get set. Enjoy!

Chapter 1

First Serve

We're serving, so finish off that banana, sip that last electrolyte and make your way to the baseline.

Lob, volley, smash, spin or dink – the ball will soon be in your court.

Are you ready to return to sender?

The greatest tennis players
in history have all had their own
nickname...

Rocket Man
Andy Roddick

Baron von Slam
Boris Becker

Can't-miss-Swiss
Martina Hingis

The Crocodile
René Lacoste

The Serbinator
Novak Djokovic

FedEx(press)
Roger Federer

Jannik The Merciless
Jannik Sinner

Fräulein Forehand
Steffi Graf

Ivan the Terrible
Ivan Lendl

Ice Borg
Björn Borg

Ice Princess
Chris Evert

Raging Bull
Rafael Nadal

The Punisher
Andre Agassi

Navrat the Brat
Martina Navratilova

Pistol Pete
Pete Sampras

Superbrat
John McEnroe

"

If people don't like my grunting, they can always leave.

"

Michelle Larcher de Brito

The Times Online, 2009

Over the years there have been scores of famous grunters, all of whom have grunted louder than 90 decibels – as loud as a hairdryer.

Today, the loudest grunter in the world is Portuguese player Michelle Larcher de Brito. Her grunt is 109 decibels, as loud as a motorcycle!

During the match against Aravane Rezaï at the 2009 French Open, Larcher de Brito's "shrieking" got so loud she was booed off the court.

"

Back then, when you were 20, if you hadn't won a grand slam by then you were almost too old!

"

Martina Hingis

CNN Sport, November 2017

Sweet Sixteen

In 1997, Swiss 16-year-old Martina Hingis became the youngest player ever to become No. 1 and the youngest person in the Open Era to win a Grand Slam singles title.

Hingis retired in 2017, claiming: "I've always loved to play tennis. This is what I do best; this is what I know; this is my education since I was two years old."

Arthur Ashe won the 1968 U.S. Open, 1970 Australian Open and the 1975 Wimbledon final. He was not only the first black player in the game's history, but the first Grand Slammer too. Ashe's game against Jimmy Connors is considered the most famous upset in a Wimbledon final – dismantling the then-world's best player.

"

Start where you are. Use what you have. Do what you can.

"

Arthur Ashe

Days of Grace, 1993

In 1988, Germany's Steffi Graf's became the first tennis player in the game's history to win all four Grand Slam titles plus the Olympic gold medal in the same calendar year, an achievement known as the Golden Slam.

66

I play every match as if it is my last, but that one, in that setting, with that history, that expectation, that tension, the rain interruptions, the darkness, the number one against the number two, both of us playing at the top of our games.

99

Rafael Nadal

Considered the greatest match in tennis history, Roger Federer's epic dogfight against Rafael Nadal at the Wimbledon final in 2008 was a five-set nail-biter. Nadal won 6–4, 6–4, 6–7 (5–7), 6–7 (8–10), 9–7. The match lasted four hours and 48 minutes, the longest singles final in Wimbledon history. *My Story*, 2012.

"

Everyone cheered, even the royal box. I did a few somersaults and a moonwalk. Officials came at me with red blankets, so I feigned being led off, and then made a run for it and dived over the net. Streaking's naughty in a Benny Hill kind of way, but it's not a crime.

"

Mark Roberts

One of the most famous match interruptions in Wimbledon's history, Roberts was a streaker who revealed all on Centre Court in the 2002 final between Lleyton Hewitt and David Nalbandian,
The Guardian, June 2015

All-Time
Game-Winning Streaks #1:
Women

1. **Martina Navratilova**, 74 (1984)

2. **Steffi Graf**, 66 (1989)

3. **Martina Navratilova**, 58 (1986)

4. **Margaret Court**, 57 (1972)

5. **Chris Evert**, 56 (1974)

6. **Martina Navratilova**, 54 (1983)

7. **Steffi Graf**, 46 (1988)

8. **Steffi Graf**, 45 (1987)

9. **Chris Evert**, 42 (1975)

10. **Martina Navratilova**, 41 (1982)

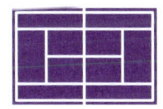

7 July 2013

The day that Andy Murray finally won Wimbledon, beating Novak Djokovic 6-4, 7-5, 6-4. More than 17 million people watched the match on TV.

After the win, Murry said:
"I understand how much everyone wanted to see a British winner at Wimbledon and I hope everyone enjoyed it. That last game will be the toughest game I'll play in my career, ever."

The Open Era

Established in 1968, the Open Era of tennis arrived when major tennis tournaments, including Wimbledon and the U.S. Open, allowed both professional and amateur players to compete together. Prior to this, amateurs and professionals played in separate tournaments.

This change revolutionized the sport, increasing its global appeal, professionalism and prize money.

491 minutes
(8hrs 11mins)

The time it took American John Isner and Frenchman Nicolas Mahut to finish their final set in the world's longest ever tennis match – 11 hours and 5 minutes! John Isner* won 6–4, 3–6, 6–7 (7–9), 7–6 (7–3) with the final set rising to 70–68!

Overall, 980 points were played in total and more than 123 balls were needed.

* The game is also famous for John Isner's record-breaking aces – 113! – the most ever in a match.

Ace of Spades

The players with the highest number
of career aces.*

1. **14,470**   **John Isner** (United States)

2. **13,728**   **Ivo Karlović** (Croatia)

3. **11,478**   **Roger Federer** (Switzerland)

4. **10,261**   **Feliciano López** (Spain)

5. **10,237**   **Goran Ivanišević** (Croatia)

6. **9,074**   **Andy Roddick** (United States)

7. **8,879**   **Sam Querrey** (United States)

8. **8,858**   **Pete Sampras** (United States)

9. **8,445**   **Milos Raonic** (Canada)

10. **8,138**   **Ivan Ljubičić** (Croatia)

* As of October 2024

Tenez

The origin of the word "tennis" comes from the French "tenez", a form of the verb "tenir", which means to hold, receive or take.

In the game's earliest form, a server would call out "Tenez!" to indicate to their opponent that they were about to serve.

Greatest Rivals

Tennis is renowned for its inspiring rivalries, showdowns that make for legendary games. These are the 10 fiercest rivalries of the Open era:

1. Roger Federer vs. Rafael Nadal (16–24)
2. Rafael Nadal vs. Novak Djokovic (29–31)
3. Novak Djokovic vs. Andy Murray (25–11)
4. John Connors vs. John McEnroe (14–20)
5. Andre Agassi vs. Pete Sampras (14–20)
6. Martina Navratilova vs. Chris Evert (37–43)
7. Steffi Graf vs. Gabriella Sabatini (29–11)
8. Venus Williams vs. Serena Williams (12–19)
9. Ivan Lendl vs. John McEnroe (21–15)
10. Billie Jean King vs. Virginia Wade (22–9)

17

The age of German Boris Becker when he became the youngest player ever to win a Wimbledon title in 1985.

The Great Upset

Shocking tennis upsets make for great television. In 2013, the greatest shock-win of the Open era occurred when Ukrainian Sergiy Stakhovsky defeated Swiss Roger Federer in the second round of Wimbledon 2013: 6-7 (5-7), 7-6 (7-5), 7-5, 7-6 (7-5).

At the time, Federer was the No. 1 player, the greatest grass player of all time and the defending champion. Stakhovsky was ranked 116 in the world.

68%

The percentage of worldwide tennis fans who consider Wimbledon to be tennis's best tournament, according to the *Daily Mirror*, 2022.

"

I'm a great lover of Wimbledon's traditions and everything they stand for but I wanted to go where no champion had ever gone before. Suddenly, there was nothing or nobody who was going to stop me. I looked up to the players' box and so many people who meant so much to me were there. I had to be up there with them. I was going to show my gratitude and climb up to them.

"

Pat Cash

Cash was the first person to climb into the trainer's box after winning the final in 1987, a tradition that several winners continue, *Pat Cash Uncovered*, 2002

1,250 Racquets*

According to Rafael Nadal's racquet maker, Babolat, the player has used more than 1,250 racquets in his tennis-playing career, as well as 54,000 overgrips and 186 miles of string!

*Unlike his peers, like Djokovic or Federer, Nadal has never once smashed or broken a racquet in anger or frustration while on court.

66

If I had asked anybody in 1985,
'Can I win Wimbledon?' the advice
would have been no. And I think
99 per cent of people would have
said it's impossible to defend it
when I was 18. But I did it.

99

Boris Becker

The Guardian, May 2023

Racquet Rage

Some of the most memorable meltdowns
in tennis history.*

1. Marcos Baghdatis – Australian Open, 2012
2. Fernando Gonzalez – Indian Wells, 2009
3. Kristos Vliegen – Monte Carlo Rolex Masters, 2009
4. Grigor Dimitrov – Istanbul Open, 2016
5. Novak Djokovic – Shanghai Masters 1000, 2012
6. Roger Federer – Miami Open, 2009
7. Novak Djokovic – Davis Cup, 2016
8. Nick Kyrgios – Cincinnati, 2019
9. Stan Wawrinka – U.S. Open, 2013
10. Coco Vandeweghe – Australian Open, 2017

*Well worth a Google.

In 2022, Wimbledon voted on its top 10 most memorable moments.

These are the winners:

1. Andy Murray's 2013 win, the first male Briton to win in 77 years.

2. Goran Ivanišević win as a wildcard in 2001.

3. John McEnroe's diabolical "You cannot be serious!" rant in 1981.

4. Pat Cash climbing into the trainer's box after winning in 1987, the first to do so.

5. Boris Becker winning as an unseeded 17-year-old in 1985.

6. The five-set men's final between Björn Borg and John McEnroe in 1980.

7. The longest ever tennis match – between John Isner and Nicolas Mahut in 2010.

9. Rafael Nadal beating Roger Federer in an epic battle in 2008.

10. Cliff Richard performing "Singin' in the Rain" on Centre Court, 1996.

All-Time
Game-Winning Streaks #2:
Men

1. **Björn Borg**, 49 (1978)

2. **Björn Borg**, 48 (1979)

3. **Guillermo Vilas**, 46 (1977)

4. **Ivan Lendl**, 44 (1981)

5. **Novak Djokovic**, 43 (2010)

6. **John McEnroe**, 42 (1984)

7. **Roger Federer**, 41 (2006)

8. **Jimmy Connors**, 37 (1974)

9. **Jimmy Connors**, 36 (1975)

10. **Roger Federer**, 35 (2005)

330 million

The amount of tennis balls* made worldwide every year, according to the *Economic Times*, September 2023.

* A tennis ball takes more than 400 years to decompose, FYI.

"

I was lucky enough to set a few records in my career, but they just happened because I played well for a long time, but when I realized I was in with a chance of breaking the Wimbledon singles record, it became a big goal of mine.

"

Martina Navratilova

Daily Telegraph, 2010

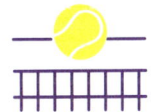

Jeu de Paume

The origins of tennis history date back more than 800 years, to the 12th century, and to Northern France.

There, bored monks developed a game in which they hit a ball over a net to an opponent with their palms.

They called it *jeu de paume*, or game of the palm.

The Tennis Court Oath

The French Revolution owes tennis a debt of gratitude, for it was a tennis court near the Palace of Versailles, that the *Serment du Jeu de Paume* (or the Tennis Court Oath) was sworn on 20 June 1789, by the leaders of the French Third Estate, a union of the three social classes in France at the time.

They vowed on this day to kickstart a new constitution for the country. It was the beginning of the end for the gluttonous monarch King Louis XVI, who ultimately lost his head.

It was the American icon Billie Jean King who won the first major, Wimbledon in 1967, using a racket made out of steel, the first time that a racket not made from wood had won a Grand Slam.

It was the Wilson T2000, FYI, and became the de facto racquet for players after King's win.

20
minutes

The amount of time
a tennis ball is actually
in play during a
standard 2½ hour
match.

Greatest Grand Slammers:
Women

24 – Margaret Court

23 – Serena Williams

22 – Steffi Graf

19 – Helen Wills

18 – Chris Evert, Martina
Navratilova

12 – Billie Jean King

 9 – Maureen Connolly, Monica
Seles

 8 – Molla Mallory, Suzanne
Lenglen

* As of October 2024.

Wild Card

Goran Ivanisevic is the most famous wildcard entrant in tennis history.

In 2001, he won Wimbledon, the only time a wildcard has won a Grand Slam tournament. He beat Australian Pat Rafter 6-3, 3-6, 6-3, 2-6, 9-7.

He was ranked 125 at the time.

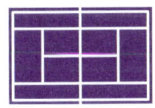

66

From the moment
I took the court and hit
the first ball, I felt I was
gliding. I was on a cloud.
It was a terrific feeling.

99

Jimmy Connors

On winning the U.S. Open Final, *New York Times*,
September 1974

Chapter 2

15-Love

And we're off! First point to you. About 150 more points to go (slightly less for a woman's game, of course), based on average game data.

You'll discover even more thrilling facts like that in this next chapter.

Serve's up!

Rain, Rain Go Away

1931, 1976, 1977, 1993, 1995, 2009, 2010, 2019.*

* Only eight Wimbledon Championships have had no rain interruptions in 102 years (since 1922).

"

Tennis is a perfect
combination of violent
action taking place
in an atmosphere of
total tranquillity.

"

Billie Jean King

All In: An Autobiography, 2021

157.2 mph

(253km/h)

The official* fastest serve in men's tennis, as clocked by American John Isner during a first-round match against Australian Bernard Tomic at the Davis Cup 2016.

* The unofficial, but still recorded, fastest serve in men's tennis is Australian Sam Groth's 263.44 km/h serve during the Busan Challenger event in South Korea, 2012. Yet to be beaten.

Germany's Sabine Lisicki has the fastest official serve in women's tennis.

At the 2014 Bank of the West Classic tournament in Stanford, U.S., she walloped an ace at 131 mph (210.8 km/h).

Greatest Grand Slammers:
Men

24 – Novak Djokovic

22 – Rafael Nadal

20 – Roger Federer

14 – Pete Sampras

12 – Roy Emerson

11 – Rod Laver

11 – Björn Borg

10 – Bill Tilden

8 – Fred Perry, Ken Rosewall,
Ivan Lendl, Andre Agassi

*As of October 2024.

"

Being a tennis player was my hobby, and then that became my job, then tennis was my identity – but it was not what I was doing all day every day. I always tried to not identify myself just purely as a tennis player. And I think that mindset has anyway been a strength of mine throughout my career. I knew that if tennis ends tomorrow, which it can, it happens, you have to be able to live with yourself without the game.

"

Roger Federer

GQ, March 2024

66

I'm sure there will be other things in life that I will grow to love, enjoy and become motivated by. But right now? I still love tennis.

99

Andy Murray

The Sunday Times, June 2024

66

You can't be serious, man. YOU CANNOT BE SERIOUS. That ball was on the line. Chalk flew up. It was clearly in. How can you possibly call that out? Everybody knows it's in in the whole stadium. And you call it out? You guys are the absolute pits of the world, you know that?

99

John McEnroe

Wimbledon chair umpire Edward James punished McEnroe with a penalty point. However, McEnroe won the game in straight sets – and the Grand Slam, 22 June 1981

54,250

The amount of tennis balls used during the two-week Wimbledon championships in 2024, over the course of 764 matches.

Bagel

The colloquial
term
for winning
– or losing –
a set 6–0.*

* A Double Bagel is two sets to love.

> ❝
> ## Only the ball should bounce.
> ❞

The now-iconic, and infamous, tagline to Anna Kournikova's lucrative brand endorsement for the Berlei Shock Absorber Sports Bra in 2000.

This provocative advert made Kournikova the highest-paid female athlete at the dawn of the new millennium.

> ❝
>
> Of the tenetz to winne or lese
> a chase, Mai no lif wite er that the
> bal be ronne.
>
> (Whether a chase is won or lost
> at tennis, Nobody can know until
> the ball is run.)
>
> ❞

John Gower

The first known appearance of the word "tennis" in
English literature was written by John Gower in his
poem titled "In Praise of Peace".

"

I can read a situation and see the look on Mike's face and I know every shot he can hit and when he's gonna hit it, and where. The communication we have, there's nothing like it.

"

Bob Bryan

The most successful doubles* pairing in tennis history is the Bryan twins, Bob and Mike. Together they have won 119 tour titles, 16 Grand Slam doubles titles and two Olympic gold medals and were ranked the No.1 male doubles team in the world for nine years, *San Diego Magazine*, May 2014.

* Fascinatingly, Mike is left-handed, Bob is right-handed.

Ice Borg

The 18-16, fourth-set tiebreaker between the brash American John McEnroe and the cool Swede Björn Borg at the 1981 Wimbledon final is now considered one of the most thrilling 22 minutes of tennis ever.

Borg lost the tiebreak but won the fifth set and the match 1-6, 7-5, 6-3, 6-7 (16-18), 8-6. In doing so, he won his fifth straight Wimbledon title!

King of the Clay

Spain's Rafael Nadal is perhaps the most iconic clay player in the history of the game.

After announcing his retirement at the end of 2024, Nadal had won 14 French Open titles – an exclusively clay terrain – the most victories by any player at a single Grand Slam event in history.

"

Tennis is a completely
different game when
you go into court and
you have nothing to lose.
Anybody can play then.

"

Boris Becker

The Guardian, May 2023

"

It's not my fault, the way I look. Yes, it's nice to have some of the attention I have, but I want to be known first and foremost as a great tennis player.

"

Anna Kournikova

Kournikova never won a singles title, though with Martina Hingis as her doubles partner, she won Grand Slam titles in Australia and WTA Championships. They called themselves the "Spice Girls of Tennis". *Esquire, July 2000.*

You Cannot Be Serious

John McEnroe's wealth of court outbursts are legendary. Here are some of our favourites:

1. "You can see as well as... these fucking flowers. And they're f**king plastic!"

   (to a line judge at the U.S. Open, 1980)

2. "I'm so disgusting, you shouldn't watch. Everybody, leave!"

   (to the crowd at the Queen's Club, 1981)

3. "You'll be sorry you hit me, you f**king communist a**hole!"

   (to Czech player Tomas Smid, 1983)

French is the most romantic language in the world, so it makes perfect sense that its footprint is all over tennis.

The origins of "love" – or nil – originates from "0" as it resembles the appearance of an egg. The French word for egg is *l'oeuf*, which sounds a lot like "love" if you really ham up the French accent.

66

Roger Federer is the most beautiful man to watch play tennis. The most beautiful I've ever seen play. His movement, combined with the artistry, his racquet, the look, he's got *everything* going.

99

John McEnroe

Wimbledon 2012

"

Tennis is just
chess – but at 90 miles
per hour.

"

Robin Williams

tennis.com, June 2009

Time for Tennis

Tennis's "15–30–40" scoring system is perhaps the strangest in all sports, but there is a method in its madness.

In the 15th century, as the game spread throughout the ruling elite of French courts, players would often use clocks to keep score. Each player began at 0, or 12 o'clock, and travelled clockwise with the small hand.

Forty was used instead of 45 as a way to accommodate for deuce – a player would move from 40 to 50 and then 0 again for the win by the two clear points players require.

> **"**
>
> Keep those balls in play, don't just give up on them, no matter how far you gotta run, chase 'em down, you never know who's going to miss a shot.
>
> **"**

Rod Laver

ABC Radio Australia, January 2023

66

Fact of the day. It takes Stefanos Tsitsipas* twice as long to go to the bathroom as it takes Jeff Bezos to fly into space. Interesting.

99

Andy Murray

Greek player Tsitsipas is notorious for taking multiple lengthy toilet breaks during his matches, X.com, November 2021

Rene was a French tennis player of great renown in the late 1920s, winning the Davis Cup in 1927. His nickname, "the Crocodile", after how much he dismantled his competition, became the icon of his clothing brand, Lacoste. He pioneered the stylish polo shirt in 1929 – the original tennis white, and the first sports-casual leisure wear.

"

Without elegance, playing and winning are not enough.

"

René Lacoste

Tennis, 1928

66

The serve-and-volley tennis is a lost art. Now everyone plays the same way; there's just four or five guys that are a lot better than the rest. For the most part it's just everyone staying back and throwing rocks.

99

Pete Sampras

Inside Tennis, January 2014

8

The precise height in millimetres of the grass* at Wimbledon, the world's largest lawn tournament.

* The species of grass is Lolium Perenne, or rye grass, the most commonly used for sports turf.

"

For me, men's tennis and women's tennis are two separate sports. If I were to play Andy Murray, I would lose 6-0, 6-0 in maybe 10 minutes. The men are a lot faster and they serve harder, they hit harder, it's just a different game. I love to play women's tennis. I only want to play girls, because I don't want to be embarrassed.

"

Serena Williams

Late Night with David Letterman, August 2013

❝

So I grunt because growing up,
I liked this tennis player named
Monica Seles and she grunts, she
had this really cool grunt. And
I loved that, I was like that's so
cool and so I would literally grunt
because of her and then it just
became natural.

❞

Serena Williams

Hot Ones, July 2024

66

On the court, on clay,
I felt like no one was
going to beat me.

99

Chris Evert

New York Times, June 2024

Britain's Andy Murray is the only male player in tennis history to have won two Olympic gold medals (London 2012 and Rio 2016) in the singles category.

Even more impressively, they were on two different playing surfaces – grass and hard court.

Breadstick

The colloquial
term
for winning
– or losing –
a set 6–1.

* The "1" looks like a breadstick.
** Surely it should be called a baguette?

I was a seven-year-old boy in Serbia watching the bombs fly over my head. Constructing a Wimbledon trophy out of any material I had in the room. Watching myself in a mirror. Telling myself I'd be a Wimbledon champion one day. Wimbledon has always been a childhood dream for me. To play – and to win it.

Novak Djokovic

On-court interview after winning his Wimbledon 2024 semi-final

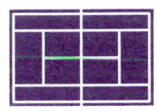

50%

The percentage of tennis players, according to data from the National Institute of Health 2020, that will develop symptoms of lateral epicondylitis, or Tennis Elbow.

This is an inflammation of the tendons that join the forearm muscles on the outside of the elbow due to repetitive wrist and arm motions.

Chapter 3

30-Love

Two points to you! Nice. If you keep this up we'll be scoffing a bagel in no time.

It's break point, so let's mix things up to keep things interesting. You'll find all sorts of spicy secrets lobbed at you in this next chapter, so feel free to come to the net if you start to spin out.

"

I'm a very positive thinker, and I think that is what helps me the most in difficult moments.

"

Roger Federer

ATP Tour, November 2018

Pulp

The colloquial term for 30–30. It's not quite deuce.*

* A pun on the pronunciation of deuce, which sounds like "juice".

28,000 kilograms
(27 tons)

The amount of strawberries consumed during Wimbledon 2024.* In recent years, strawberries and cream have become synonymous with this summer tournament.

During the two week competition, every morning before dawn, scores of pickers arrive at Hugh Lowe Farms, Kent, to cherry-pick strawberries – more than 1.5 million in total – to fill the 140,000 bowls of fresh strawberries and cream served to spectators every day.

*With approx. 10,000 litres of cream!

❝

I loved tennis, but I didn't want that life anymore.

❞

Björn Borg

After winning five Wimbledon and six French Open
titles, Swedish champion Borg quit the game aged 26,
blaming the intense fame he received, claytenis.com,
May 2023

Tennis is responsible for many English metaphors and phrases we all use every day – all set, aced it, game, set and match, straight down the line, break point, tie-breaker, unforced error, grand slam and gain advantage, for example.

The most popular one, of course, is "the ball is in your court", to mean "your turn to make a decision".

It rose to popularity in early 19th century when lawn tennis started to become an internationally popular leisure activity.

"

To me, tennis was always just being on court. I loved the playing and I loved the training. I enjoy performing before a crowd, even though you wouldn't know it from my face or my body language. I took the game the only way I knew how – seriously – and it wasn't in my personality to be smiling on the court or getting involved with the crowd.

"

Steffi Graf

Sportstar, April 2020

66

What a polite game tennis
is. The chief word in it seems
to be 'sorry' and admiration of
each other's play crosses the
net as frequently as the ball.

99

J. M. Barrie

"Tennis", The Boy Castaways of Black Lake Island,
1901

Everyone can win when they're playing well. That's not the difficult part of the game. It's when you're playing average tennis, you find ways to get through.

Andy Murray

usopen.org, August 2023

When players are not preparing for Grand Slams, they are training for the 64 tennis tournaments, across 31 countries, that comprise the Association of Tennis (ATP) Tour and Women's Tennis Association (WTA), which includes historic trophies such as the Davis Cup, the Laver Cup, The Miami Open and Indian Wells.

All players must play at least 21 tournaments a year.

66

Tennis teaches you how to cope
with everything you're going to
have to deal with in life – stress,
lack of confidence, figuring out
how to perform, how to come back
if you fail. Athletes do make better
choices in those moments.

99

Venus Williams

Harper's Bazaar, September 2024

MOP

The term used when a player scores two consecutive points, or 0–30.

Stands for:
Major Opportunity Point.

The home of the world's stunning bright red clay courts is at Stade Roland-Garros in Paris, and has been since 1928. Clay is considered a tricky surface as it causes the ball to bounce higher and slower than any other surface, but it makes for great sliding!

The French Grand Slam tournament is named after the war hero and aviator Roland Garros, the first-ever man to fly solo over the Mediterranean.

66

Victory belongs to the most tenacious.

99

Roland Garros

There are only five players in the history of the game who have won a Career Golden Slam.

This includes all four major Grand Slam titles and Olympic Gold medals.

They are:

Steffi Graf (1988)

Andre Agassi (1996)

Rafael Nadal (2010)

Serena Williams (2012)

Novak Djokovic (2024)

Prize Money

Female tennis players with the highest career earnings in million U.S. dollars, according to Statista 2024.

1. 94.82 – Serena Williams
2. 42.60 – Venus Williams
3. 40.20 – Simona Halep
4. 38.78 – Maria Sharapova
5. 37.25 – Petra Kvitova
6. 36.65 – Victoria Azarenka
7. 35.55 – Caroline Wozniacki
8. 31.89 – Angelique Kerber
9. 27.68 – Agnieszka Radwanska
10. 25.82 – Svetlana Kuznetsova

> "

It's one-on-one out there, man. There ain't no hiding. I can't pass the ball.

"

Pete Sampras

Tennis Creative, June 2022

> **"**
>
> My whole mission in life was playing tennis. What are you doing today? Practice. What are you going to do? Train. And if you get injured, what are you doing today? Rehab. And that had been my life for over 40 years.
>
> **"**

Serena Williams

New York Times, June 2024

"

I feel like everybody on the top
level plays great tennis, but it's
those who can mentally cope
with the most stressful moments
who are the champions.

"

Iga Swiatek

Poland's 23-year-old prodigy and regular
world No.1, Iga has already won five Grand Slam titles,
including the U.S. Open and the French Open,
Vogue, August 2023

The U.S. Open

Welcome to the U.S. Open at the USTA Billie Jean King National Tennis Centre, Flushing Meadows, Queens, New York, where this hard court tournament is hosted every year.

Played on DecoTurf (an acrylic-topped surface), the championship is famed for its medium-fast pace of play, making it ideal for a wide range of playing styles.

The U.S. Open hosted possibly one of the most thrilling matches of all time, the 2001 quarter-final between two legendary rivals – Pete Sampras and Andre Agassi.

With every set going to a tie-break and neither player being able to break serve, it was Sampras who eventually won: 6-7, 7-6, 7-6, 7-6.

"It was probably as good as it gets, playing the very best in a night match at the U.S. Open," Sampras said after. "The atmosphere was phenomenal, and it was so close."

9 July 1877

The date of the inaugural , and oldest, tournament: Wimbledon Championship at the All England Club, Worple Road, Wimbledon.

In 1877, 22 gentlemen competed for the Singles event, with 200 spectators paying one shilling each to watch the final. Former Harrow student Spencer Gore triumphed over William Marshall 6–1, 6–2 and 6–4, in 48 minutes.

Gore won prize money of 12 guineas, around £2,000 in today's money.

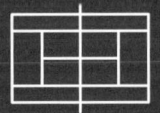

Golden Set

The term to describe a set that is won without dropping a single point.

A Golden Match is when a player does not lose a single point in the entire match.

This happens rarely at a professional tournament.

"

Tennis is a sport where things can change very quickly. That's the great beauty of it.

"

Rafael Nadal

CBS News, May 2021

"

I remember the very first time I had to walk onto court. I was really nervous. And my producer in my ear, suddenly said, 'Sue Barker, walking out, just the estimated 500 million people watching you right now. Good luck!' That wasn't the best thing to say as I was wandering out with my microphone!

"

Sue Barker

The world's most beloved tennis commentator and former player, Barker retired from the BBC in 2022 after 30 years, Virgin Radio, June 2024

Grand Slam

The U.S. Open, the French Open, the Australian Open and Wimbledon are the four major tournaments in tennis.

They are known as Grand Slam tournaments.

If a player wins all four major tournaments in the same year it is referred to as a Grand Slam.

If a players wins all four, but not consecutively in their career, it is called a Career Grand Slam.

Only a handful of players have
achieved these feats including
eight men and ten women.

Fred Perry	Maureen Connolly
Don Budge	Doris Hart
Roy Emerson	Shirley Fry Irvin
Rod Laver	Margaret Court
Andre Agassi	Billie Jean King
Roger Federer	Chris Evert
Rafael Nadal	Martina Navratilova
Novak Djokovic	Steffi Graf
	Serena Williams
	Maria Sharapova

317,520

The number of glasses of Pimm's* served at Wimbledon 2024.

This is the equivalent of three 25-metre swimming pools' worth!

* For those that don't know, Pimm's is gin infused with a secret combination of herbal botanicals, caramelised orange and warm spices.

Brutaliser

The colloquial term for when a player hits the ball directly at their opponent.

Prize Money

Male tennis players with the highest career earnings in million U.S. dollars, according to Statista 2024.

1. 181.60 – Novak Djokovic
2. 134.66 – Rafael Nadal
3. 130.59 – Roger Federer
4. 64.35 – Andy Murray
5. 43.28 – Pete Sampras
6. 39.95 – Alexander Zverev
7. 39.30 – Daniil Medvedev
8. 36.65 – Stan Wawrinka
9. 31.48 – David Ferrer
10. 31.30 – Marin Cilic

1972

The year that tennis balls became yellow (changing from white).

They were introduced by American Mike Davies, the then-executive director of the World Championship Tennis Tour. He knew yellow balls would be more visible on a smaller screen with the advent of colour television.

Davies told the BBC in 2014: "If tennis wasn't on television, it wasn't going to be a major sport in the world."

I just thank God I played the game long enough to enjoy lots of good moments. It gave a lot and it took a lot. I think me and tennis are about even now.

Andre Agassi

The Guardian, March 2017

66

I've often told people that
I feel in my heart the French
Open in '89 was one God
wanted me to win.

99

Michael Chang

On 11 June 1989, American Chang beat Swede
Stefan Edberg to become the youngest ever French Open
champion at 17 years old, *New York Times*, May 2023

"

Tennis teaches you to not quit until the match point is finished. I don't know if you're born with it, or if you learn it later, but it definitely becomes a habit.

"

Martina Navratilova

Piers Morgan Uncensored, March 2023

532,651

The number of spectators who got tickets to watch matches at Wimbledon 2023 – the largest in the championship's history.

Chapter 4

40-Love

Welcome to the MOP!
This is the match opportunity
point you've been waiting for.

This is usually when the
big guns come out to finish
opponents off, so consider
this chapter the greatest hits
of tennis trivia – the ace in
the hole...

In 1995, British player Tim Henman and doubles partner Jeremy Bates became the first players in the Open Era to be kicked out of a tournament after Henman accidentally hit Caroline Hall, a ball girl, in the head. Per tennis rules, if a ball person is hit during a match and is hurt, the player or team is disqualified. UK headlines the next day claimed Henman hit the ball girl so hard "it could have killed her".

To apologise, Henman gave Hall a bunch of flowers and a kiss on court. In 2008, Hall told *The Guardian*. "Nothing was meant by it at all, it was just bad timing that meant the ball hit my head instead of going into the net."

"

Even though there is no physical contact in tennis, there's still a lot of eye contact... And then I'm looking at him. How is he drinking water? Is he sweating more than usual? Is he breathing deeply or not deeply? You have all these different elements that are in play that really affect the performance and the game itself.

"

Novak Djokovic

CBS News, August 2024

First Winners

Wimbledon (1877)
Spencer Gore

U.S. Open (1881)
Richard Sears

French Open (1891)
H. Briggs

Australian Open (1905)
Rodney Heath

New Balls!

At Wimbledon, new balls are introduced into matches after the first seven games, then every nine games after that. This allows balls to warm up, but not become too degraded from the 100mph punishment.

At the start of each day, 46 tins of balls are taken to the Centre and No.1 Courts. Used balls are available to be purchased after the matches at the Southern Village store, £2.50 for three. All proceeds go to the Wimbledon's charity foundation.

If they made grunting against
the rules, then I would have to
think about it, but otherwise
I would do whatever helped me
to play my best.

Monica Seles

The Guardian, July 2009

For 15 years, officials at the All England Lawn and Tennis Club have employed Rufus, a Harris Hawk, to keep an eye on the skies during Wimbledon – and reduce the ever-increasing pigeon problem.

However, during Wimbledon 2012, Rufus was stolen from the back of a car. The news made global headlines and Rufus was labelled "the world's most famous bird".

He was found three days later. The thief remains unknown.

"

My generation was the last
when you were marketed
really as a tennis player.
But when Anna Kournikova
came along, there was this
whole other thing – suddenly
it was all about looks.

"

Monica Seles

The Guardian, July 2009

"

I don't know any other person
that has won a Grand Slam
or a championship in the NBA
or anything else nine weeks
pregnant.

"

Serena Williams

Time.com, August 2022

Before and after every tour game
and Grand Slam tournament,
the ATP (men's tennis association)
and WTA (women's tennis
association) rank players based
on their performances.

Points are earned through wins,
with more prestigious tournaments
offering higher points. Rankings
determine seeding in tournaments
and qualification for prestigious
events like the ATP finals and
WTA finals.

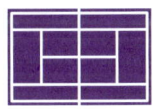

> I think the rivalry with Boris Becker has been very good for both of us, because that's really what's important in tennis. We've been fighting through Wimbledon and we've been fighting for the No. 1 spot and looking at each other's results.

Stefan Edberg

The Independent, June 1996

The Australian Open

Revered around the world as the "Happy Slam", the Australian Open is the first Grand Slam of the year and has welcomed all of the all-time greats. Like the U.S. Open, its surface is a hardcourt and plexicushion, perfect for a medium-paced, low-bounce game.

The venue gave witness to the most brutal game in recent history: the 2012 final between Novak Djokovic and Rafael Nadal. Djokovic won 5-7, 6-4, 6-2, 6-7, 7-5, but it was a six-hour showdown.

"

This one was very special...
But I really understand that was a
really special match, and probably
a match that's going to be in
my mind not because I lost, no,
because the way that we played.

"

Rafael Nadal

Reflecting on the 2012 Australian Open final

Royal Tennis

Before the advent of "lawn tennis", the precursor to the modern game, there was "real tennis", the first of its kind to use racquets.

Akin to squash, "real tennis" was played indoors and used walls as part of its court. The game gained immense popularity among European royalty, especially in France and England.

King Henry VIII (1509-1547) loved the game and built Britain's first tennis court at Hampton Court Palace to prove it. You can play there today.

Major Walter Clopton Wingfield, a British Army Officer, and "father of lawn tennis" wrote the book on the sport and is credited with popularizing his version of the game in 1873, adapted from indoor "real tennis".

He patented his game, calling it "Sphairistikè". He invented an hour-glass court shape and sold portable sets, which included racquets, balls and a net, allowing people to play it at home.

He also wrote detailed rules, that were refined in 1877 ahead of the first ever Wimbledon, drawing heavily from Wingfield's vision.

"

The game was so slow back then. I've watched Boris Becker... a big serve back then was like 197km per hour. People like me, we serve 220 consistently, to corners. It's a whole different ball game.

"

Nick Kyrgios

New York Times, December 2023

> The young players who are hungry and inspired to play their best tennis against me is an additional motivation. They awaken a beast in me.

Novak Djokovic

CBS News, August 2024

The Sport of Kings

King James I (1394–1437) of Scotland loved tennis, but tennis was also, quite literally, the death of him.

The king grew so sick of losing tennis balls down a sewer drain at the corner of the court he played on, at Blackfriars Monastery, that he ordered the drain to be sealed.

Unfortunately, when assassins came to capture him in 1437, the King fled down the sewage drain only to find it sealed off – and full of tennis balls.

Racquet/Racket

The origin of the word "racquet", or "racket", derives from the Old French word "rachette", which was a paddle-like tool used for scraping barnacles off the bottom of a ship in the 1300s, according to the *Oxford English Dictionary*.

Racquets weren't commonly used until the 1600s.

Next time you watch the prize ceremony at the Wimbledon final, look closely at the top of the Gentleman's golden trophy. Atop sits a pineapple.

Even today, no one is really sure why!*

* Some believe it has to do with pineapples being a symbol of high status during the Victorian era of Britain, when the trophy was first devised.

In 2001, American powerhouses Venus and Serena Williams broke history when they met at the Grand Slam final of the U.S. Open.

It was the first time that sisters – and two people of colour – had played the tournament's final.

The match lasted 69 minutes. Venus won 6-2, 6-4.

3 miles

During a match,
a professional player will,
on average, run more
than three miles – and
burn as many as 3,000
calories.

"

The size of the racquet heads,
the materials used, the strings
are all very different today,
contributing to the hard edge
of the game, which frankly
has replaced the finesse that
used to be a hallmark of tennis.
Today it's a power game, all
for television, and all about
the money.

"

Roy Emerson

LA Times, May 2017

20 September 1973

The date of the famous "Battle of the Sexes" match between Billie Jean King and Bobby Riggs.

Riggs, a self-proclaimed 55-year-old chauvinist*, believed he could beat King in her prime. The match was watched by tens of millions. King defeat Riggs in straight sets, 6–4, 6–3, 6–3.

As a result, the U.S. Open became the first Grand Slam tournament to offer equal prize money* to men and women.

* In 1972, when King won the women's U.S. Open singles final, she was awarded $10,000, while the men's singles champion received $25,000. King boycotted playing the U.S. Open until the prize money was equal, a threat that led to Rigg challenging King.

American player Tracy Austin was just 16 years and eight months when she beat the legendary Chris Evert at the 1979 U.S. Open 6–4, 6–3.

It's an achievement yet to be beaten.

66

Blue is better on the eye than green. I think it's important that you see the ball properly on TV.*

99

Roger Federer

The New York Times, 2007

* The hard court surface of the U.S. Open turned blue in 2007 to help players and fans better see the yellow tennis ball. The precise shade is Pantone Blue 2965U.

Money Spinners

The winners of Grand Slams are handsomely rewarded:

£2.35 million – Wimbledon*

$3.6 million – U.S. Open

$3.15 million (AU) – Australian Open

€2.4 million – French Open

*The prize money for Wimbledon winners became equal for men and women, but only in 2007.

Box Set

1. Margaret Court (Australia)

2. Doris Hart (America)

3. Martina Navratilova (Czech-American)

The three players in the history of the sport to have achieved a career Boxed Set, the term applied to those that win in the singles, doubles and mixed doubles categories at all four Grand Slam events.

Deuce

Jimmy Connors, Pete Sampras and Roger Federer are tied with five U.S. Open men's singles titles – the most in the Open Era.

In the WTA, Chris Evert and Serena Williams have the most women's singles titles with six each. Which rising star will break the tie?

Red clay

Red brick dust:
1–2 mm

Crushed white limestone:
6–7 cm

Clinker (coal residue):
7–8 cm

Crushed gravel:
at least 30 cm

The composition of the bright red
clay court at Roland-Garros.

A different floor makes for a different game than the one played on grass or synthetic surfaces. Red dirt is slower, which makes for a brand of tennis which is less direct and more tactical – a veritable game of chess, where a certain shot can lead to a conclusion four or five 'moves' later.

Jim Courier

roland-garros.com

66

Tennis gave me a lot more than it took away. It gave me the opportunity to travel, get to know the world, meet the world. I was an introverted and scared person. I was paralyzed by the fear of having to speak publicly as a tournament winner and speak to the press. I could not play freely any more. My head was completely closed. Tennis helped me express myself. This sport gave me the chance to travel around the world.

99

Gabriela Sabatini

La Nacion, May 2020

Australian Margaret Court is considered one of the greatest tennis players of all time, winning 24 women's singles major titles and 64 major titles, from 1960–1977. She was also a priest.

"

I loved my tennis days,
I believe it was a gift from God.

"

Margaret Court

The Telegraph, September 2022

Chapter 5

Game, Set, Match

Welcome to victory!
You won the match point!

Congratulations.
Time to raise the golden
trophy. Just try your best
not to drop it like
Carlos Alcaraz did at
Wimbledon 2023.

We'll see you again. Our
rivalry has only just begun...

"

I am really proud to see where the sport is now, from where I started, to see how it transcends through culture, through fashion and art, it now brings together so many people from different walks of life – and to have played a small part in this makes me feel great.

"

Maria Sharapova

Harper's Bazaar, July 2024

> ❝
>
> We're from the ghetto. Venus is a ghetto Cinderella. People from the ghetto don't get nervous.
>
> ❞

Richard Williams

The father of Venus and Serena Williams, *Newsweek*, September 1994

Olympic Champions

The United States has more tennis Olympic gold medals than any other nation.

1.	United States	21
2.	Great Britain	17
3.	France	5
4.	Germany	3
5.	Russia	3
6.	Switzerland	3
7.	South Africa	3
8.	Spain	2
9.	Czech Republic	2
10.	Chile	2
	China	2

5.9 million

The amount of new tennis players regularly enjoying the sport in America.

Tennis has surged in popularity since 2020 and the aftermath of the pandemic – 33 per cent increase, according to *Forbes* magazine, January 2023.*

*The same is also true of the UK, with a 43 per cent surge in enthusiasm for the sport, an additional million players, since the pandemic.

4:33am

The time the latest ever match concluded in 2008.

The five-set thriller between Australian Lleyton Hewitt vs Cypriot Marcos Baghdatis lasted four hours and 45 minutes but play did not start until 11.45pm. Hewitt won 4-6, 7-5, 7-5, 6-7, 6-3.

Hometown Glory

When a player wins a tournament at home, the whole nation goes bonkers:

French Open
Yannick Noah, 1983
Mary Pierce, 2000

Australian Open
Ashleigh Barty, 2022
Mark Edmondson, 1976

U.S. Open
Andy Roddick, 2003
Coco Gauff, 2023

Wimbledon Championship
Andy Murray, 2016
Virginia Wade, 1977

"

I feel like I won the match before I even stepped on the court.

"

Coco Gauff

Gauff won the 2023 U.S. Open and is the next generation player to keep an eye on, time.com, April 2024

66

The trouble with me is that every match I play against five opponents: umpire, crowd, ball boys, court and myself.

99

Goran Ivanisevic

During the Samsung Open in 2000 Goran famously smashed all his available tennis rackets while playing a match.

Sydney 2000
Beijing 2008
London 2012

The Olympics at which doubles partners, and sisters, Serena and Venus Williams, have won gold medals.

The first and only time in history.

Let

The origin of the word "Let" in tennis is derived from the Old Saxon word *lettian*, which meant an obstacle.

In tennis, a let is an obstacle to the smooth flow of play.

Queen of the Hard Court

Serena Williams was the hardest opponent to defeat on hard courts throughout her career, winning a combined 13 Grand Slam titles on the surface – seven Australian Open titles and six U.S. Open titles.

With her power and aggression, hard courts suited Serena's game best... but of course she was pretty successful on grass too, winning Wimbledon seven times!

"

There was a little extra motivation
that year because of the Queen's
Silver Jubilee and the fact that it
was Wimbledon's centenary year,
and maybe fate played a part
as well. The Queen was going to
be there, and that was enough
motivation to say, 'If she's going to
be there, I'm going to be there too.'

"

Virginia Wade

The last British woman to win Wimbledon (1977)
and the only British woman to win four Grand Slam
tournaments, *The Guardian*, June 2007

The next point – that's all you must think about.

Rod Laver

lavercup.com

King of
the Hard Court

With a record 10 Australian Open titles (the most at any Grand Slam on hard courts) and four U.S. Open titles, Novak Djokovic has dominated hard courts for 20 years. The surface allows his stamina, flexibility and tactical prowess to shine.

In November 2023, he became the first man to win 40 ATP Masters 1000 titles in the Paris Masters, all played on hard court.

Queen of the Grass

If you're looking for the most iconic grass player in the world, stop. Because it's Martina Navratilova.

With 167 singles titles to her name – and 177 doubles – from 1974 to 2006, Navratilova was simply unbeatable, winning on Wimbledon's lawn a record-breaking nine times – including six singles in a row from 1982-87 – a feat that probably will never be beat – plus seven doubles and four mixed doubles to boot.

"

There is nothing like playing at Wimbledon; you can feel the footprints of the legends of the game – men and women – that have graced those courts.

"

Venus Williams

The Times, June 2006

King of the Grass

This crown belongs to Roger Federer – without a doubt!

He's been victorious on Wimbledon's lawns more than another other gentleman – eight titles: 2003-2007, 2009, 2012, and 2017.

His footwork and strokes of genius are particularly suited to the fast-paced, low-bouncing nature of grass courts.

71,000

The number of tennis clubs globally. The highest number of clubs – 17 percent – are in the United States with Germany second on the list, with 13 percent.

Tennis clubs are where new stars are discovered and old stars go to coach.

* According to the International Tennis Federation (ITF) 2019 Global Tennis Report, the first global report and the most comprehensive accumulation of modern tennis data.

66

– 50 million children started
playing tennis
– 5 million learnt to play tennis
– 500,000 learnt professional tennis
– 50,000 came to circuit
– 5,000 reached Grand Slam
– 50 reached Wimbledon
– 4 reached the semifinals
– 2 reached the finals
And when I was holding the cup in my
hand, I never asked God: 'Why me?'
So now that I'm in pain how can I ask God:
'Why me?'

99

Arthur Ashe

On his deathbed after suffering from AIDS, 1983,
replying to a fan letter that asked, "Why did God have
to select you for such a bad disease?"

King Richard

In 2021, director Reinaldo Marcus Green made one of the most poignant father-daughter movies in recent history.

With tennis at its heart, the story tells the early life and sacrifice of Serena and Venus Williams through the eyes of their dedicated dad, Richard, depicted by Will Smith.

The film was a massive success, and won Smith his first Oscar, deservedly so.

Top 10 Tennis Movies

Suspense. Intrigue. Drama. Victory. Defeat. Sex. It comes as no surprise that Hollywood loves making tennis movies. Here are the greatest hits:

1. ***Battle of the Sexes***, 2017
2. ***7 Days in Hell***, 2015
3. ***Wimbledon***, 2004
4. ***The Royal Tenenbaums***, 2001
5. ***Challengers***, 2024
6. ***Match Point***, 2005
7. ***Balls Out***, 2009
8. ***The Computer Wore Tennis Shoes***, 1969
9. ***Borg Vs McEnroe***, 2017
10. ***King Richard***, 2017

66

Nobody beats Vitas
Gerulaitis 17 times in
a row.

99

Vitas Gerulaitis

Gerulaitis finally won after Jimmy Connors
had defeated him 16 times in a row, ATP Finals,
January 1980

66

That moment on the court, when I was celebrating, I was like, I would literally trade any struggle in the world for this moment. Anything can come my way, I will take it for what I have right now because this is the best thing in the world. And sometimes I think to myself I wish I'd never won the U.S. Open, I wish that didn't happen.

99

Emma Raducanu

Raducanu stunned the sports world when she triumphed at the U.S. Open 2021 aged 19 – the first British woman to win a Grand Slam singles title since Virginia Wade at the 1977 Wimbledon Championships, *Sunday Times*, June 2023

34 minutes

The total time taken for German Steffi Graf to defeat Belarusian Natasha Zvereva in the 1988 French Open final, 6–0, 6–0.*

It is the shortest ever Grand Slam match in the Open era. (It was actually all over in just 32 minutes of playing time but there was a short rain break.)

* This match is the only double bagel Grand Slam singles final of the Open Era.

Britain's first ever tennis court, at Hampton Court Palace, was built for the young monarch, King Henry VIII in 1526. The king loved tennis almost as much as he loved executing his wives.

Indeed, on 2 May 1536, his second wife Anne Boleyn was arrested – on charges of adultery, incest, and treason against Henry – while watching a game of tennis at London's Whitehall.*

* She was transported to the Tower of London and beheaded two weeks later.

Deuce

The term comes from the French phrase *deux de jeux*, meaning two games.

Deuce can only be settled when a player wins two points consecutively.

1 March 1913

The year tennis went global when National Tennis Associations from separate nations came together to create the International Tennis Federation (ITF), the governing body of world tennis, in Paris, France.

According to its manifesto, the ITF works hard to "maintain and enforce the rules of tennis, regulate international team competitions, promote the game, and preserve the sport's integrity," as well as oversee annual team competitions for men and women, and tennis events at the Summer Olympic and Paralympic Games.

> "

I'm one point away from serving for it. He had a second serve. And I was thinking to myself, Just double-fault. And he double-faulted. I couldn't breathe on the next switchover. I'm like, This is it. It's yours now. I think I fired three or four aces. Just unconscious.

> "

Andy Roddick

Roddick is the last American male to win a Grand Slam, the U.S. Open 2003 against Spain's Juan Carlos Ferrero. It was the only Grand Slam title of his tennis career, GQ, August 2024.

66

When I was a 15-year-old in that semi-final at Wimbledon, I definitely thought it was an easy game. I've discovered that nothing – the game, life, anything – is as easy as it was back then.

99

Jennifer Capriati

She lost to Steffi Graf in the semi-final
at Wimbledon 1991, *The Guardian*, June 2003

"

I have these two sayings, 'Champions adjust' and 'Pressure is a privilege'. Tennis teaches you about those things. When you're playing a tennis match, you can't say, 'Stop, I want to do another take', or 'Can I play that over?' That's the way sports are.

"

Billy Jean King

Daily Express, October 2008

The Davis Cup

Beloved as the "World Cup of Tennis", the Davis Cup Finals is the most famous tournament after the four Grand Slam championships.

Established in 1900, and hosted in November, the Cup now sees 155 nations compete, with winners crowned World Champions. Each nation puts forward a team of five players, with each player playing a match over the course of a week.

		Wins	First	Last
1.	United States	32	1900	2007
2.	Australia	28	1907	2003
3.	Great Britain	10	1903	2015
4.	France	10	1927	2017
5.	Sweden	7	1975	1998

87,000,000

The number of tennis players globally, professional, club players and 'hit and gigglers', or non-competitive social tennis players.

China has the most players – 22.5 percent – with the United States second on the list, with 20.7 per cent.

*According to the International Tennis Federation (ITF) 2019 Global Tennis Report, the first global report and the most comprehensive accumulation of modern tennis data.

489,135

The number of tennis courts worldwide. The highest number of courts belong to America with 16 per cent, with China ranked second in the list with 10 per cent.*

* According to the International Tennis Federation (ITF) 2019 Global Tennis Report, the first global report and the most comprehensive accumulation of modern tennis data.

Queen of the Clay

Ladies and gentleman – Chris Evert. This iconic American player won the French Open seven times, more than any other female player.

In her 15 year career, she spent 260 weeks as world No. 1, won 18 Grand Slam titles and had a clay court match record of 382 wins (only 22 losses).

That's a 94.55 percent win-rate!

Number One No. 1

Since 1975, 29 women have been ranked No. 1 in singles by the WTA. However, Steffi Graf is the undisputed G.O.A.T of being No. 1.

She holds the record for being the female tennis with the most number of weeks ranked at the top spot – 377!*

* For the men's game, Novak Djokovic is the record holder – 428 weeks.

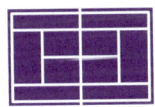

66

It's quite overwhelming when you are an American and your lifelong dream comes true.

99

Lindsay Davenport

On her spectacular U.S. Open win in 1988, usopen.org, September 2020

66

Tennis started off as my
hobby and now it's my job.
But it's important I still play
like it's my hobby.

99

Jannik Sinner

Italian superstar Sinner is one of the sport's most
recognisable rising stars. He won the 2024 Australian
Open and U.S. Open and is seen as the future of the
men's singles game. *The Guardian*, May 2024.

66

I'm addicted to tennis.
I'm a competitive guy when
I get on the court. I love
competing, whatever it is.
It gets the juices flowing.

99

Leyton Hewitt

Daily Telegraph, June 2018

The more I lose, the more
they believe they can beat me.
But believing is not enough,
you still have to beat me.

Roger Federer